Truth Matters: 101 Principles that Molded my Life and Ministry

Gregory R Reid

DEDICATION

To all those who selflessly poured their wisdom and love into a young preacher who was hungry for truth and direction. Your example, faithfulness, and guidance have stayed with me for a lifetime. It is my prayer that I can give to those God has given to me what you gave to me.

Introduction

We all come from somewhere. None of us is without ancestors, whether saints, scoundrels, or somewhere in-between. And much of what we are is molded by those that raised us and surrounded us growing up, for good or ill.

As believers in Jesus, we also don't get hatched out of an egg. There are people who influenced us, prayed for us, discipled us, and loved us. I was blessed to have some extraordinary men and women of God who spoke into my life as I grew in the Lord and then walked in ministry. Some of their own spiritual DNA became part of mine through the words they shared and the lives they lived, by their examples and the codes they lived by.

In addition, there have been a few principles I picked up from others who were not in my immediate circle of care that nonetheless became a permanent part of me. Most of these are good old solid Biblical truths, and a few are just common-sense wisdom, handed down by a generation or two that knew how important it was to live with integrity, godly values and what they used to call "horse sense."

There are many of these that God taught me Himself, and this book was written in part to hand down to those who have heard them and who will perhaps make them part of their own spiritual DNA as they seek to follow Him and His Word and allow their lives to speak to the next generation, should Jesus not return soon.

Where credit can be given, I will give credit. Where I could not find the source, I offer my apologies and a promise to include your name in later editions of this book. The principles not credited are things that God Himself taught me by His gracious hand.

I have added some comments on each principle. Some need very little commentary at all. I've included some backstory on those that need it for the principle to be properly understood, and I have tried to make that brief as well.

My prayer is that the foundational truths and common "horse sense" wisdom I share here, that became the framework of my faith and calling, may also become part your own foundation in Christ or principles of ministry. May they serve you well, as they have me.

Gregory R Reid

October, 2019

ONE

Don't Ask Why. Ask What For.

Our very human cry when we are hurt, or life is unfair and people cruel and unkind is to say, "Why, God?" Jesus taught me early on to ask, "What for?" instead. "What is this meant to do in me, Jesus, how is it meant to change me, and how do I submit and respond to Your will in this painful time and awful circumstance?" He wastes nothing. "Why's" only lead to despair. "What for's" give Jesus the opportunity to teach us, strengthen us, change us, love us. (Ro. 8:28)

TWO

Throw Your Hat Over the Wall

(Frank O'Connor)

Irish writer Frank O'Connor told the story of two boys standing beside a tall orchard wall launching a small, felt, round object up in the air like a Frisbee. "If you had been there to see them, it would have looked strange—even foolish. With the enthusiasm of a college graduate, one of the boys hurls his hat, and you arrive just in time to see it leave the hand of its owner and travel high—up and over an imposing and significant wall. You might have wanted to call out and say, 'Why did you do that? Now you are going to have to climb over and get it!' To which, the boys would reply with sly and knowing grins, 'Exactly. That's the whole idea.'"

President John F. Kennedy referenced this story in 1963 when speaking of his commitment to space exploration despite the dangers and many unknown factors. He explained how O'Connor and his friends "would make their way across the countryside, and when they came to an orchard wall that seemed too high and too difficult to permit their voyage to continue, they would take off their hats and toss them over the wall—and then they had no choice but to follow them." Kennedy then applied this to the nation and declared that the United States had now "thrown its hat over the wall of space and had no choice but to follow it."

We may call it "stepping out of the boat," like Peter stepped out, or climbing an impossible cliff with one other person thinking he could defeat an entire battalion of soldiers like Jonathan, or any other number of things that speak of *outrageous faith and actions* in the Bible, actions where the person had to "throw their hat over the wall" in faith so they had no choice but to climb it to get their hat back.

May God make us people of outrageous faith and great courage that if we feel God gives us a mission, we will do it with reckless abandon to our God who never fails those who act in faith.

"Without faith it is impossible to please Him." (Hebrews 11:6)

THREE

Your Life Is Your Ministry

(Roger Lengyel)

People are always talking about full-time ministry. But my friend who gave me this believed that whatever you were doing, and whoever you were with, *was* your ministry. Yes, there are people who pastor churches, do missions work, and other "full time" ministry work. But every believer is called to ministry, and what you do, and *who you are*, and how you share Jesus with others *is* your ministry.

"Whatever you do, do it heartily, as unto the Lord, and not unto men." (Colossians 3:23)

FOUR

This Life is Just the Dress Rehearsal for Eternity

(Rick C Howard)

This life is short, and everything we do and say is meant to conform us into the image of Jesus, and everything God does and allows is to fit us to rule and reign with Him for eternity. Let go of the insignificant, the trivial and the temporary; focus on eternal things. Make every moment count. Use everything as preparation to prepare you for forever.

Everything we do and say matters. Everything we do and say has consequences for good or bad, and for the believer, everything we do and say here on earth – the dressing room - is what prepares us for all that is to come in the Great Eternal Then.

FIVE

God Doesn't Always Pay On Fridays

(Rick C Howard)

Evil is real. Injustice, unfairness, corrupt people, and painful betrayals are part of what we have to live with as believers in this broken, sinful world.

People don't play fair. The greedy and the ambitious are often allowed to cut in line and shove out the weak and vulnerable, crushing their dreams. And sometimes, as a good friend says, it seems like "no good deed goes unpunished."

Jesus warned us so we wouldn't be caught off guard. "In the world you will have tribulation, but be of good cheer. I have overcome the world." (John 16:33) Don't be surprised that good things happen to bad people, and bad things happen to good people. And don't be unsettled because it seems like everybody gets away with it all. "God doesn't always pay on Fridays." We will all stand before God and account. And one day, God will make all things right. "The wheels of God grind slow, but they grind exceedingly fine."

SIX

Nothing to It But To Do It

(Vic Richards)

Hermano Victor was one of my first spiritual mentors and fathers when I went into full-time ministry. He and his wife Gloria were always there and always available to me as I navigated all the challenges of ministry, people, and God's plan for me.

Many times I struggled with just basic things I knew needed to get done: Fixing a broken relationship, exercise, and diet, dealing with seemingly impossible challenges. This simple answer has stayed with me for a lifetime: "Nothing to it but to do it." Stop putting things off, just tackle it now and get on with the rest of what you have to do.

Feel challenged by all the things you have to do, putting off harder things hoping they will go away or you will feel more able to tackle it tomorrow? Just grab it, jump in, and get it done.

Nothing to it but to do it!

SEVEN

If It's Doubtful, It's Dirty

(Doris Shumate)

It's an old school expression, vintage Ashville NC smoky mountains wisdom via my spiritual mother. In times when I was debating whether I should engage in certain things, like going to a party "for Jesus" or whether to date someone, the principle she laid out here was pretty clear: If I have to ask whether something is something I should do, if I hesitate and feel uneasy, I need to stop and ask God why. And it may be that the Holy Spirit is saying, "Don't do this." I need to listen to His voice and keep my foot from a trap. "If it's doubtful, it's dirty." If my conscience is warning me, I need to stay away from whatever it is my flesh wants me to do.

EIGHT

If All Our Problems Were Hung on a Line, You'd Take Yours, and I'd Take Mine.

(Doris Shumate)

Again, this is pure Smoky Mountain wisdom, from a time when people hung their washed things outside on a laundry line – this is their version of, "The grass isn't greener on the other side of the fence." We may think we'd like to be in another person's shoes, their job, their fame, their family situation, their financial state, etc. But you don't see or feel their problems and their hurts or their fears and their struggles. And if you did have them for a moment, you'd say, "That's ok, I'll take what's on my plate."

NINE

Fear Knocked; Faith Answered. There Was Nobody There.

(Old English Proverb)

Fears will always come and go. When they come, we must treat them as an enemy, and faith is the enemy of fear. "Perfect love casts out all fear, because fear has torment." (1 John 4:18) Fear has no power until we give it power by giving into it. Put your faith in the Lord Jesus Christ who rose from the dead to deliver us from fear of death and the grave, and proclaim the truth, "God is at work in all things to produce good for those who love him." (Romans 8:28)

"What time I am afraid, I will trust in You." (Psalm 56:3)

TEN

Two Lessons in Roadbuilding and Team Playing

(Claudette Stewart/Rosemary Beugler)

Claudette and Rosemary were two godly women in their late 40's that were called of God to travel 70 miles one way twice a week from their homes in Dennison, Texas, to teach a bunch of kids at Christ for the Nations in Dallas how to sing in sign language and be part of a tiny deaf ministry, Signs of Love. (I wrote more of their story in my book, "Stray Cats and Other Stories.") It cost them nearly everything to carry out that work. I loved them like mothers in the Lord.

One day in my second semester, I caught them crying in the tiny prayer room on campus. They let me know that the Lord had told them He was sending someone on campus to take over the ministry. They would know him when they saw him – and they were to give him the ministry and walk away, and that person would take the Signs of Love around the country and even around the world.

I was stunned and upset. "How can you just give up your ministry like that?" I protested in my youthful naivete about how things work in God's kingdom. In words I will never forget, Rosemary said, "Oh, Darlin, it's not our ministry. It's always been God's." "But all the work and prayer and love you put into it!" I continued, feeling the grief of seeing these dear ladies leave us, and maybe never return. "Hon," Claudette continued, "**There are those that build the roads, and those that travel on them. Those that travel on them will never know what went into building the road. But all that matters is that it is a smooth, good road**. I think we've done that." But what will others think? "**We always play for the coach, not for the crowds**."

Many years have passed, and I too have had to give up or walk away from pioneer works. When the heartbreak and tears came, I remembered these golden words. I did my best to make it a good, smooth road before I left, and though others often did not understand, I turned my eyes toward the Coach and away from the crowds, praying that He will be pleased and one day I might hear the words I long to hear: "Well done, good and faithful servant."

ELEVEN

You're Either a Saint, or You Ain't

(Unknown)

Many believers, particularly young believers, struggle in their faith, and when failures come, or they fall into sin, they wonder, "Am I really saved?" It is a great time to be reminded that your salvation is not dependent on you, or how much or how little you sin. "By grace you are saved through faith; and that not of yourselves; it is the gift of God, not of works lest any man should boast." (Ephesians 2:8-9)

In other words, it's not conditional or by degrees, a little saved or a lot saved. You're either a saint, or you ain't. And if you are, it's not because of what you do but what He already accomplished in full. We are saints not by earning but because He proclaimed us to be so and purchased our salvation at the cost of His precious blood.

TWELVE

Don't Touch the Girls, Don't Touch the Gold, and Don't Touch the Glory.

(Via Pastor Scott Hayes)

Three very wise words of advice were conveyed from an older preacher to a younger one when asked what the most important things to remember about going into ministry were.

In an age when scandal, financial excess, and self-promotion seem to be the things modern evangelical and Charismatic leadership has way too much of, it is good to remember these sage words. Flee sexual temptation at all costs. Live modestly, not like a corporate executive with all the perks. And remember that all that God does through you has nothing to do with you. You are just a vessel, nothing more in His work.

"Giving no offense in anything, that the ministry be not blamed." (2 Cor. 6:3)

THIRTEEN

Be Who You Is, 'Cause If You Ain't Who You Is, You Is Who You Ain't.

(Unknown)

If you just be the person God created you to be, instead of trying to impress people with how cool you are, you can become the person you're meant to be instead of building a façade of a person you aren't.

What does hypocrite mean? "One who hides behind a mask." A play-actor, playing a role and hiding behind that mask.

Years ago, I asked one of the kids in our youth ministry what his best advice was for me. He said, "Don't blow your class." In other words, don't try to look or act like anyone you are not. If you do, everyone is going to know it, and you'll lose real "authenticity."

Just be who you is. "By the grace of God, I am what I am." (1 Corinthians 15:10)

FOURTEEN

The Broken Wing

(Doris Shumate)

My spiritual mother told about a hymn she had sung in her church as a young person that spoke of a bird that had gotten caught in a snare and broken its wing and was never able to fly as high as it did before.

It just didn't sit right with her, the grim message that if you were a believer and you sinned or strayed, though you returned to the Father, you would never fly as high as you did before. She wrote the author a letter, suggesting that when the Father healed, that little bird might actually fly higher than it ever could before because God does all things well. The author changed the song.

We all sin and fail. Satan often traps us under condemnation, convincing us that we can never again be who God intended because of our disobedience and sin. Remember the prodigal son. Come home. Be restored, and fly higher than you could have ever dreamed because of His goodness, healing, and grace. "There is forgiveness with thee, that thou mayest be feared." (Psalm 130:4)

FIFTEEN

Jesus is Either Lord of All in Your Life, Or He Isn't Lord At All

(Dave Malkin)

Jesus doesn't want part of your life. He wants absolutely everything, every day, for the rest of your life. Anything less is not being a disciple. He may be your Savior, but He isn't your Lord if you still run your life your way.

"Why do you call me Lord, Lord, and do not do what I say?" (Luke 6:46) That is a question we must ask ourselves if we truly want to claim Him as our Lord.

SIXTEEN

If You Hear Hoofbeats, Don't Think a Zebra is Coming. It's Probably Just a Horse

(Betty Reid)

My mother had an understanding that we all tend to fear the worst and let our fears create wild scenarios of awful things that could or might happen. Most of the time, nothing turns out as terribly as we fear. This simple bit of wisdom has often kept me from assuming the worst and fearing the most horrible outcomes of things and made me laugh in the process.

"There were they in fear, where no fear was…" (Ps. 53:5)

SEVENTEEN

All That Matters Is That Which Is Eternal

(Amy Carmichael)

Nothing has grounded me more than this simple statement. In the end, the only thing that will remain is what will count for eternity – not wealth, not prestige or position, not popularity or fame. Just what we have invested in the Kingdom to come.

EIGHTEEN

See in It A Chance to Die

(Amy Carmichael)

Amy Carmichael, the missionary to India whose writings have most influenced my own writing, spoke of having been wronged by another believer, and how the Lord spoke to her these clear words when she was unsure what to do with that wrong.

We too are often faced with these dilemmas, with people, circumstances and unexpected hurts and disappointments. In all things, when our flesh wants to react, lash out, get even, hurt back, and any number of other "human" responses, these words are golden advice: SEE IN IT A CHANCE TO DIE. No matter how hard, or how much it hurts. Look to Jesus and the cross, who for the joy set before Him – the joy of buying us back from sin and death that we might be His forever – endured the cross. We too will face our painful crosses, and at that moment make the decision to either turn from that cross and handle things our own way, or see in that circumstance, that awful cross or loss, a chance to die – to our self-will, our pride, and our flesh. Welcome the cross knowing healing and resurrection are on the other side.

"We who are strong ought to bear the infirmities of the weak and not to please ourselves." (Romans 15:1)

NINETEEN

Put the Glass Down

(Unknown)

The first time I attended Bible School, I was confused and scared, not sure I could complete the semester. I was scared to leave and scared to stay. I arranged to get counseling from one of the professors. He was kind, patient, and a good listener.

While I was talking, he showed me a jar full of water, dirt, and rocks.   While I poured out my dilemma, he gently shook the jar. After about ten minutes, he said, "What do you see?" "Nothing," I said. "Just a mud cloud." He set the jar down and kept listening.

When I was done, he took the jar down. "What do you see now?" To my amazement, I saw every layer of sand, rock, and water perfectly.

"When you're in fear and upset," he explained, "Nothing is clear. Just cloudiness and confusion. You need to set the jar down for a while, stop worrying. Worship and love God and read the Word. Let go of the fears and trust Him. Before long, it will become very clear what God wants you to do."

I did, and He did. From that time on, whenever I find myself tied in knots and unable to see clearly, I just set the jar down and immerse myself in the Lord and His Word.

And the answers have never failed to become clear.

"Cast all your care upon the Him, for He careth for you." (1 Peter 5:7)

TWENTY

Periphery

(David Wilkerson)

I was incredibly blessed that my spiritual life began with brother David Wilkerson's book *The Cross and the Switchblade*, which was the deciding moment in me coming to Jesus.

When I got into ministry, I was further blessed to be asked by David to accompany them in a weeklong evangelistic outreach in San Francisco. He supported my small work for some time.

He came to our town for a crusade, and I had arranged to meet with him and ask for prayer and counseling. We talked of many things, but what he said that stayed with me was discussing struggles with sin and temptation. "If you have sins and temptations on the periphery of your heart, God will give you victory if you seek Him. But if a sin becomes the center of your heart, that is when you are in grave danger."

It was very clear to me that I must never (only by His grace) allow any sin to take the place that is reserved for my Jesus – the throne of my heart.

TWENTY-ONE

God Is Never Late, but He Misses a Lot of Opportunities to Be Early.

(Dan Sattelmeier)

Sometimes it's the simple things put in a funny setting that stick with you the most. Pastor Dan is one of my favorite preachers and teachers, and he always had a way of framing truths in memorable ways. This was one of them. And it's true. God never, ever fails. But usually, He's right at the edge of midnight! And through this, I understood that this is one of the ways that God increases our faith and trust. Thanks for the reminder, pastor!

"Wait on the Lord, and be of good courage, and He shall strengthen your heart. Wait, I say, on the Lord." (Psalm 27:14)

TWENTY-TWO

It Isn't Vessels of Gold He Desires. It isn't Vessels of Silver. It's Yielded Vessels.

(Katharyn Kuhlman)

We live in an age of easy and "bless me" Christianity where so many are into it for what they can get out of it. Kathryn Kuhlman, whom God used to do so many mighty miracles, understood the secret of brokenness and yielding to God 100%.

God isn't looking for you to be gold or silver vessels, just surrendered vessels, that He might fill you with His Spirit and use you in any way that He may choose.

"We hold this treasure in earthen vessels, that the excellency of the glory might be seen to be of God, and not of us, that no flesh should glory in His presence." (2 Cor. 4:7)

TWENTY-THREE

It's How You Finish

(Rick C Howard)

Rick is my spiritual father, a man who took me under his wing and took a risk on this very young preacher when I was just 22 and not just invited me to preach, but kept asking me back. I still am astonished that he kept having me back since in the beginning, I could not seem to preach under 90 minutes! (I've gotten much better!)

The first time I heard Rick preach, I was riveted to the seat. He was clear, truthful, and pulled out the stops. It molded and informed my own heart and ministry. God chooses well.

Although I have heard many dozens of Rick's messages, the one that remains with me is "Finishing the Course," a powerful recalling of Stephen's short life, and a vulnerable perspective of fighting the good fight of faith, even when every bone in your body is screaming to quit.

Rick used a lot of sports references – as did Paul. Football was the main reference in Rick's sermon. His message, among other things, was that games aren't won in the first quarter. Determine to be a great 4th quarter believer.

Because although the whole race is important, we stumble, we get weary – but what matters the most is *how you finish*.

"I have fought a good fight, I have finished my course, I have kept the faith." (2 Timothy 4:7)

TWENTY-FOUR

Jesus said, "Without Me you can do nothing." Unfortunately, without Him, in our flesh, we can do plenty.

Beware the plague of busy work meant to just make us feel like we are accomplishing something for Jesus. Without Him, nothing we do is any more than window dressing and a show. With Him, we can do amazing things. Just make sure they are His things, not ours.

There used to be a cynical bumper sticker that said, "Jesus is coming back. Look busy." I laughed because that described many believers I knew that felt like the more they did, the more impressed Jesus would be – not to mention others who marveled at their industrious labors in the Kingdom.

But only those things that Jesus commissions you to do will remain and bear fruit.

TWENTY-FIVE

Promotion Comes from Above

(Charles & Audrey Mieir)

Audrey Mieir was a little lady with a big heart who called herself a "little fat Polish-Irish mother" without one ounce of self-denigration, and she won my heart. She was a legendary songwriter, and her songs, "His Name is Wonderful" and "To Be Used of God became hymns for the ages.

She had brought her choir, "Audrey Mieir and Her Recording Choir" to our little Foursquare church to sing and to raise money for their mission to adopt Korean-American children who had been abandoned after the war.

At seventeen I was still ridiculously shy, but I knew I had a call from God, and I knew I wanted to speak with Audrey, so I slowly made my way to the stage and talked to her for quite a while.

We stayed in touch. I supported their mission as much as a 17-year-old could, and Audrey, in turn, wrote notes and cards to say thank you and to encourage my young heart in pursuing ministry. What followed that meeting turned out to be a lifetime relationship with Audrey and her amazing husband, Charles, and in between letters and counsel, I sometimes made the journey to their hometown in Duarte, California, and shared a meal – and usually a hot fudge sundae – (Audrey's favorite) with them as I poured out my heart, my concerns, my struggles in ministry once I went full in. The hours of love, prayer and godly counsel will stay with me forever, and although Audrey and Charles have stepped into the Forever Kingdom, their words of counsel remain the backbone of God's character building in me.

Audrey gave me a wonderful bit of wisdom, coming from Psalm 75:6 when I was struggling about wondering *how* to promote my ministry, or even if I should. Other ministries and ministers, especially big and well-known ones, used all kinds of promotional tricks to get recognized. Should I?

"Promotion doesn't come from the east or the west," Audrey said lovingly. "Promotion comes from above. Never promote yourself. Let God do the promoting. He will open all the doors He wants you to go through."

From that point on, I made a diligent effort

not to promote myself. And God has been faithful to open every door for me. I would rather trust and make sure that HE is opening the doors rather than open them myself and never be sure if God was in that promotion.

He's the best ministry manager there is!

TWENTY-SIX

Life Is in the Moments

It seems like our entire lives are spent getting from point A to point B. Hurry up and graduate from High School. Finish up college. Get married, have children. Get a great job, save money for retirement. And then die.

And in the process, we miss some of the most precious moments we will ever have because we are not looking for them. We are so busy filling all our moments that we miss the moments that matter the most.

Life is not in the accomplishments; it is not in the prestige; it is not in the goal setting or meeting those goals. It is in the moments we have with each other and with Jesus – those moments when time seems to stop and we are sharing something with each other that is so priceless, so eternal that you know it will not come again.

So slow down. Take a deep breath. Ask God to give you eyes to see and ears to hear so that when those unrepeatable, irreplaceable moments happen, you will not miss them. You will stop and embrace them

– and those who bring them.

Life is but a vapor, a wisp, here and gone like the morning smoke from a chimney on a cold winter's day. Do not miss the gifts God wants to give you every day in the ordinary, in the routine, in the moments. They will not come again.

"Redeeming the time, because the days are evil." (Ephesians 5:16)

TWENTY-SEVEN

God Is in Control

(Tim Gamwell)

Tim was my partner in ministry for several years. I've never met a calmer, steadier believer. He was always involved in crisis situations, life and death situations, situations that most believers – even many ministers – were reluctant to tackle. And no matter how radically bad the situation was, he never failed to offer one bit of truth in the midst of the other counsel he might have offered, no matter how out of control a situation might be – simple, direct and absolutely true. "God is in control." If we can make that part of our bedrock of faith, then no matter how crazy or difficult or painful or hopeless a situation might be, we will never be moved from the rock that is Jesus Christ.

He will never fail us.

TWENTY-EIGHT

God Has No Second Plans

In our human thinking, that tends to make God in our own image and likeness, we somehow believe that if we miss God's direction or miss a turn in His plan, he has to go to "plan B," as if He is somehow caught off guard and says, "Oh, no! I didn't see that coming! NOW what? I guess I'll have to come up with a second plan for them." I think part of this thinking has come from a misreading of Romans 12:2: "And be not conformed to this world but be ye transformed by the renewing of your mind, that ye may prove what is that good, and acceptable, and perfect will of God." There were even teachings about the differences between the good and acceptable and perfect will of God, and you would often hear people say, "It wasn't God's perfect will," as if there was a lesser one He was ok with. But the verse is only saying that God's will is good, and acceptable, and perfect.

In fact, He only has one plan. And if we manage to do something to divert from that plan or even run from it like Jonah did, the good news is, He already knew. And He already has a redemptive plan in place for it. One plan. One perfect plan. He is the ultimate chess player – He always checkmates us. And as one person says, the King always has the last move!

"For I know the thoughts that I think toward you, saith the Lord, thoughts of peace, and not of evil, to give you an expected end." (Jeremiah 29:11)

TWENTY-NINE

Stay Sweet

Many of us when we came to Jesus were filled with a joy and peace we had never known. We experienced the love of Jesus and that of others that was real, tangible, and life-giving.

Nothing remains that simple. People being people, and sin nature being what it is, we soon get knocked around and injured, betrayed, and treated ugly, and we are shocked, and we are sad. And that's just the stuff we experience from other believers! Don't be shocked. The Gospels, the Book of Acts, and the Epistles are full of incidences and references to such things. Even Paul said, "Alexander the Coppersmith did me much evil." (2 Tim. 4:14)

We can't keep the ugly things, the personal wounds or the shattering behavior of others from happening (and we often are just as capable of being the cause of such things.)

What we can do, in all circumstances, is to stay sweet. Even if it hurts, stay sweet. Even when we've been misunderstood, stay sweet. Even when we feel betrayed, treated unfairly, abandoned, stay sweet. Bitterness is a root that dearly loves a wounded heart. Don't ever let it take root. Forgive until it hurts, give it to God when your guts are screaming to God for recompense, and even when your broken heart is crying for just some kind of recognition of the wrong done. Let it go, God knows, He sees. A broken heart is more precious to Him than gold. Remember that His Son never opened His mouth but like a sheep before his shearer, went to His death on the cross without speaking a word in anger or judgment, but simply, "Father, forgive them, they know not what they do."

Stay sweet no matter how brutally you feel the slings and arrows of others' words and actions. Better to endure and stay sweet than to give in to the devil's poison of bitter resentment and unforgiveness.

"...you thought evil against me; but God meant it for good..." (Gen. 50:20)

THIRTY

How Long Does It Take to Recover? As Long As it takes.

It is so easy – too easy, really – when someone loses a loved one, either through death, separation or divorce – for us to come in and provide quick answers ("Aren't you glad they're in heaven now? God needed another angel…") You know the routine. But one of the things people often say in these circumstances is, "You should be over this by now. It's time to move on," as if we were a box of parts on a conveyer belt.

The fact is that grief and loss are hard. And yes, we have hope, especially in death that because of Jesus, this life is not the end. But Paul said, "do not sorrow, even as others that have no hope." (1 Thess. 4:13) He did not say we do not grieve. So, we need to be gentle, kind, and compassionate and not be a Job's comforter trying to dispense easy answers from a place of not suffering such a loss. Just be there. Care. Pray. Listen.

One such a person came to me and said, "How long will it take to 'get over it?' It's been three months…" I told them, "I can tell you exactly how long it will take." "Really?" they asked hopefully. "Yes. As long as it takes." And although it was not the answer they expected, it was the one they needed to hear. This grief and loss were between them and Jesus, and they needed to take all the time they needed to find healing.

God made us all differently. And every person grieves different, hurts differently, and heals differently. How long will it take for you to heal and recover? As long as it takes. And only God can determine that. Take all the time you need. Jesus will walk with you every step into His healing tomorrow.

THIRTY-ONE

Spiritual Bootcamp is All Guts and No Glory.

"Why are things so hard? I thought God had called me into ministry!" Things are hard *because* God has called you into ministry. You are in spiritual Bootcamp. In the world, no one enjoys boot camp. You are pushed to the limits of endurance. There are times you are screaming inside for it to stop. But this is how soldiers are made.

You are a soldier in the most important war there is – a war against the spiritual forces of darkness. Endure the training. In fact, embrace it, no matter how hard it is. The Father who has called you has chosen every part of this hard training to prepare you to be mighty for battle when He calls you to get in the fight.

THIRTY-TWO

I Can Learn from Criticism, No Matter How Painful.

Nobody loves criticism. Don't let it make you angry or bitter. Learn from it, and unless it is just unspeakably satanic bile spoken out of the mouths of human demons, listen, take it in and ask Jesus, "Is there any truth to this?" Change what you can that He reveals that needs changing, and discard the rest, being careful not to respond in kind just because you got your feelings hurt.

Some people launch criticism out of a bitter heart, like little kids throwing toys at someone they don't like. Be the adult and forgive them.

THIRTY-THREE

God Doesn't Show Me Others' Faults So I Can Criticize Them, But So I Can Pray for Them.

It is so easy to criticize others, especially believers when we see their weaknesses, sins or faults. It's not ours to criticize. If God trusted you let you see those things, that means you need to be trustworthy enough to pray for them, not gossip about them or esteem yourself better. "I thank God I am not as other men are," boasted the religious man in the house of God. Not far away, a "sinner" cried out for mercy. Jesus said that "sinner" was justified by God. If we see someone's sins as something to easily point out and condemn because it's not what *we* do, we're on dangerous ground. (The joke used to be that the fundamentalist's version of sin is what *you* do that I *don't*.)

No, better to pray with compassion for that person, knowing full well that the same grace that they need is the grace that redeems you, and your sins are no better than theirs. "But for the grace of God go I" may not be in the scriptures, but it definitely should define our heart-attitude toward even the "worst" of sinners.

THIRTY-FOUR

Always listen to both sides before deciding the truth of a matter.

It is too easy to take someone's side, or someone's offense, without first listening also to the person on the other side of that offense. There are always facts not yet known; we all will defend and justify our actions toward another, whether we were the one injured or the one injuring, or even both. Listen carefully to every side; then you by God's grace can be a peacemaker between people, or an arbiter of truth and help people to do right, godly things.

"He that answers a matter before he hears it, it is folly and shame to him." (Proverbs 18:13)

THIRTY-FIVE

Ministry Is Relationships

In our megachurch world, we have become a well-oiled machine with many moving parts. Unfortunately, often the sheer size of it and need for organized people and departments has left us with little room for what actually matters to God – relationships. "You need to get plugged in," I have heard it often said. But people are not appliances. They need *heart* connection. True ministry is not about delegating, relegating, organizing and "going to the next level" – true ministry is about the love of God compelling us to care for each other and for the wounded, the lost, the lonely, the abandoned, the widow, the orphan and all those in need of His love and grace and salvation in Jesus. People are not projects. Never treat people like notches on a spiritual gun belt. True ministry happens person to person, as His heart connects with ours and to another's. True ministry is organic, not mechanic. And costly. It costs *you*. And the best ministry is about lifetime relationships in Jesus with those He has given us. In true ministry, people are not replaceable cogs in a machine. They matter. They are part of us.

THIRTY-SIX

When Christ calls a man, he bids him come and die.

(Dietrich Bonhoeffer)

The way of Jesus is the way of the cross. Jesus said, "If any man will come after Me, let him deny himself, and take up His cross and follow Me." (Matthew 16:24)

Jesus came to bring us life and life abundantly, and life in Him is full of blessings. But we want the power of the resurrection without the fellowship of His sufferings. He calls us to surrender our will, our heart, our all. He calls us to die to ourselves and the old man of sin.

"That I may know Him, and the power of His resurrection, and the fellowship of His sufferings, being made conformable unto His death…" (Philippians 3:10)

THIRTY-SEVEN

The Prison Story

Another one of my spiritual fathers, John Garlock, was a great writer and a great storyteller, a man full of compassion, grace, and an awesome sense of humor. He relayed this story to me that made a deep impact on me:

A prisoner who had committed multiple murders shocked everyone one day when he walked down to the front in the prison chapel and gave his life to Jesus.

A prison minister who met him was so excited about this changed man that he convinced his pastor to go with him and meet with him. The pastor agreed.

The Pastor sat across from this former murderer and asked him about his coming to Jesus. The man took a big drag off his cigarette, accidentally blowing the smoke into the pastor's face. "I'll tell you what, Pastor," the man said excitedly. "Finding Jesus was the best @#$% thing that's happened to me in my whole @#@#^% life!"

The Pastor was furious and railed at the prison

chaplain on the way home. "I thought you told me this man was saved! And I go in there, and he blows smoke in my face and swears like a sailor! How do you explain that?!?"

"Well, Pastor," the prison chaplain said meekly, "We figured we should just get these men to quit murdering people and go from there...."

We are all saved at different places and circumstances in our lives, from different backgrounds, and struggling with different sins. It would be wonderful if we all just were perfected the moment we got saved. But we aren't. (See Principal 38) Some immediately stop doing major sins, some struggle with them. Some struggle with outward sins, some hidden sins of the heart not easily seen. Only God knows our hearts. Let's not be too quick to judge another based on their post-Christ behavior. Give them grace, and time - as you want God to give it to you.

THIRTY-EIGHT

We *have* been saved from the penalty of sin. We *are* being saved from the power of sin. And one day, we *will* be saved from the presence of sin.

(Unknown)

This simple principle is a clear view of "sanctification." Our sins are forgiven completely, past present and future, by Jesus' death on the cross. The power of sin is being broken in our lives daily as we walk with Him in His Word and in fellowship with others. And blessedly, we will one day cross the river into that land when sin will touch us no more, forever!

"And the very God of peace sanctify you wholly; and I pray God your whole spirit and soul and body be preserved blameless unto the coming of our Lord Jesus Christ." (1 Thessalonians 5:22)

THIRTY-NINE

We are in the same boat on a stormy sea, and we owe each other a terrible loyalty.

(G.K. Chesterton)

I know there are times that we have to disconnect from other believers when they go into serious error. I know there are also times that it may be necessary to part ways with a family member.

But in recent years, I have seen that it is far too easy for people to cut ties over small disagreements, little doctrinal issues or just because of a fight that one or the other or both are too proud to humble themselves over and mend things.

For years I have watched nasty church splits, broken family relationships, and severed friendships personally and in my own family. We even coined a phrase for it based on the old Twilight Zone program, where a little boy controlled an entire group of adults, and if they displeased him, he "wished them into the cornfield" and they ended up as a scarecrow.

Too many people, rather than doing the hard work of loving each other in the church or in our families, just wish people into the cornfield. "I won't apologize unless they do." There are so many shattered friendships and relationships in Christ because we don't have the humility or courage to be the first one to make things right.

The sea is stormy. Life is difficult and often overwhelming. Are you thinking about a broken relationship as you read these words? Do something today to make it right if you can. Don't let the day come when they are gone, and you can no longer wish them back from the place that you exiled them to.

FORTY

How to know if you are called? You can't do anything else and be happy

Just try. And if your heart and thoughts are burning with the desire to serve Jesus and others with your whole heart, obey the call and ask Jesus to open the way to fulfill that call.

FORTY-ONE

The three-text rule

This used to be a three-letter rule, before writing became extinct and we found an easier way to pour our anger and hurt on another person. Now we can text our hurts, our anger, our offenses. Or Facebook them in what they call a "passive-aggressive" fashion, knowing that the person it's intended for will probably know it's about them, but have no way of responding back. "I wasn't talking about you!"

What do you do when you get an outright nasty, angry or pain-inducing criticism or attack via email or text or even an antique letter?

First, give it to God.

Second, forgive them.

Next, write your response, holding back nothing.

Then, wait a day. Re-read it.

Then, write it again.

Wait another day, and read it one more time.

By then, hopefully, you have taken out the arrows of poison you felt and are able to respond in a godly, kind way, full of mercy and grace - even forgiveness - a response that will short-circuit the "attack-counterattack" reaction the enemy counts on to bring further hurt. You will have given God a chance to work that grace into your heart.

Don't send it until you have peace, and your sole motive is to bring His truth and healing into things.

And keep your fingers off of THE CAP LOCKS. Don't be a KEYBOARD WARRIOR. You're called to be a peacemaker if you can. And if your response is rejected, then let it go and be at peace that you did what God asked you to do.

"If it is possible, as much as it lies within you, live peaceably with all men." (Romans 12:18)

FORTY-TWO

If Satan can't get you to do one bad thing, he will get you to do 100 good things that aren't God's things.

Unfortunately, many churches are built around projects, outreaches and busy work with little emphasis on prayer, scriptures, and waiting on God for direction.

One of Satan's favorite tricks is to get you loaded up with "good things" that God didn't ask you or commission you to do, and you completely neglect or overlook the thing or things He's called you to do.

It's ok to say no. Remember Mary and Martha. Martha did many busy things but wasn't sitting at the feet of Jesus fellowshipping with Him. Jesus said. "One thing is needful, and Mary has chosen that good part." (Luke 10:42)

Do that "one thing" first; then He will lead you into those things He wants you to do.

FORTY-THREE

The Church Won't Be the Church Until It Is Willing to Get Coffee Spilled on Its Carpet.

Can we be honest? Most of us want church to be neat, clean, and pleasant, an oasis we can go to at least once a week to escape from the pressures of life, work and family and just rest.

But we are not a resort. We are a hospital. And until we are willing to let things get messy, and receive messy, broken, inappropriate socially inept, smelly, unkempt, angry, hurt, outrageously dressed people, then we're not really the church.

If we're more concerned that we don't get stains on our new carpet, then we are simply a watering hole for well-fed sheep, when we should be a 911 search-and-rescue mission for those who have been torn to shreds by wolves and devils.

FORTY-FOUR

The most dangerous prayer in the world is, "Whatever it takes, Lord, do it."

Do not pray this prayer unless you mean it, for God will hear and answer it. Whether you are struggling with a sin, asking for an answer to a difficult prayer or situation, or just simply wanting to lay your all down at the altar for the sake of Jesus and the call of God on your life, when you pray this prayer, know that God will begin to move to answer this desperate prayer. And He will do whatever it takes to move you into the center of His will. The surrendered life is the life God wants us all to live.

FORTY-FIVE

If as you get older your messages are more head stuff and less heart stuff, it's time to reevaluate your walk with Jesus.

It's so easy to resort to a file cabinet full of sermons that are already done rather than do the spiritual wrestling needed to bring a fresh Word of God to people. As we get older, it is easy to resort to old sayings, cute bromides and well-worn bits of information rather than from-the-heart fiery truth that can only be gleaned by having a heart that is close to the fire of God's heart and the altar of prayer.

Check your messages. If it's more head stuff than heart stuff, it's time to return to your first love.

FORTY-SIX

Don't ever, ever, under any circumstances date or marry an unbeliever.

"Be not unequally yoked together with unbelievers: For what fellowship has righteousness with unrighteousness? And what communion has light with darkness?" (2 Corinthians 6:14)

Is there any part of this you don't understand? It's as clear as it can be. I have seen far too many young believers ignore this crucial command and sacrifice their calling and future joy because they wouldn't trust God to bring them a godly mate.

Trust Him and don't reject this vital command. Ignore it to your own hurt.

FORTY-SEVEN

We all fall. Just make sure that when you fall, you fall toward the cross.

If confess our sins, He is faithful and just to forgive us our sins, and to cleanse us from all unrighteousness." (1 John 1:9)

A man once asked a man known to be a faithful servant of Jesus, "How do you keep walking with God so faithfully?" The humble man simply replied, "I fall down, I get up."

Only quitting is unfixable failure. If you fall, fall toward Calvary and let the Savior cleanse you and put you back on your feet.

FORTY-EIGHT

Don't ever interpret the Lord's anointing on your ministry as His approval of your personal life.

I have seen so many people over the years start out well and blessed with great anointing, big crowds, miracles and many people coming to Christ, only to learn after they fell that they were engaged in adultery, debauchery, drug abuse or financial impropriety. Yet all the time, the anointing and blessing were working through them.

Why?

First, God blesses the faith of the hearers and the proclamation of His Word. We are just vessels.

Second, Paul said, "For the gifts and calling of God are without repentance." (Irrevocable.) (Romans 11:29) That means it is entirely possible for God to use someone mightily in ministry yet have their personal lives be a shambles and end in ruin. It was truly a sobering moment for me when I read this and realized that I could be experiencing great ministry and blessings, yet be completely walking in sin and spiritual bankruptcy in my personal relationship with Jesus.

"Jesus," I prayed, "Take me out of ministry before I ever get to the point where I am living two lives."

I would rather have my walk with Jesus strong and right and have no ministry than to have the greatest ministry in the world and have my personal life be one of shame, and one that will potentially bring shame on His Name.

FORTY-NINE

Ministry is heart and tools: Let God burn in your heart that thing He's called you to do, find the tools he brings, refine them and He will do all the rest.

All true ministry comes from God birthing compassion, vision, and a driving desire to serve Him. God burdens our heart; it gestates and becomes a vision. "Write the vision and make it plain upon tables, that he may run that reads it." (Habakkuk 2:2) And that vision will bring the tools to carry out that precious thing God has called you to do.

FIFTY

If Satan doesn't attack you before God uses you, he will surely attack you after. Keep your guard up at all times.

We always expect a battle when we are doing Jesus' work – criticism, no help, discouragement, sleepless nights and a number of things the enemy does to get us off course or just get us to give up before we've got the mission done.

After, there is always a great relief, and a sense of, "I'm glad we did it, and I'm glad it's over!" That is precisely the time we need to be the most cautious. Satan is vindictive, bitter and determined. He hates God, and thus you, and if he can't get you to stop before, he tries to attack you after. Keep your armor on and your shield ready, because that's when you might experience the fiery darts of an angry enemy: "So what? Yeah, you did a little something, but you're no Billy Graham. What difference did you really make?" He's like the bully at the beach trying to kick sand in your face.

Be prepared for that attack, and confront it firmly and absolutely. Give Satan no ground, before or after. And leave the results to Him.

FIFTY-ONE

Don't be afraid to say I don't know if you don't. It's a lot better than making something up and being exposed for it later.

This takes a lot of humility. This takes a lifetime.

FIFTY-TWO

Sabbath is not an option. Ignore it at your own peril.

Paul didn't say, "Don't honor the Sabbath." He just said not to fight with people because they choose a different day to honor it.

The day of rest was designed for *us*, Jesus said. Our bodies, minds, hearts, and spirits are designed to go for six days and then STOP. I think a lot of our physical, emotional and familial issues could be cured if we would take this command seriously and honor it.

Take a day. Rest. Pray. Read the Word. Don't do errands and busywork. Spend time with your family eating, talking, sharing, mending. Stop the madness of the six-day grind. Just. Stop.

And pastors, Sundays is NOT your Sabbath. That's your work day. Find another day and take it off.

FIFTY-THREE

You can't keep birds from flying over your head, but you can keep them from making a nest in your hair.

(Martin Luther)

The biggest battle most believers, especially young believers face is the battle for their thoughts. The enemy knows this and is very good at "inserting" thoughts into our ears, trying to make us own them. But the original thought may not even be yours. So kick them out of the nest of your mind immediately, rebuke them and send them flying. A good scripture or two will do that job nicely.

Don't give them even a moment's time or a "second thought" to allow them to take root.

FIFTY-FOUR

Sin always takes you where you don't want to go, keeps you there longer than you ever wanted to stay, and makes you pay what you never thought you'd have to pay.

Sin is a deadly, seductive and determined thing. Be like the Proverbs tell us: "Surely in vain the net is spread in the sight of any bird." (Proverbs 1:17) Stay elevated in Jesus' tree. Don't let sin take you to a place you don't want to go, a place you can't afford to waste any time on and shouldn't pay another cent on. Jesus paid it all so that you would never again have to follow this slippery slope of sin.

FIFTY-FIVE

"Let my heart be broken with the things that break the heart of God."

(Bob Pierce)

Good general rule: The thing that breaks your heart is the thing you are called to do.

"How do I know what God wants me to do?"

What touches you, moves you, breaks your heart to hear about? Homeless people? Human trafficking? Broken teenagers, desperate drug addicts, abandoned elderly people?

Do that ministry. God put in your heart what is in His.

FIFTY-SIX

When about to talk about someone to someone else, ask these questions: Is it right? Is it kind? Is it *necessary?*

It's a very old expression, but how important it is. If you're not 100% sure that what you heard is true, don't say anything to others. If you aren't speaking in compassion and genuine concern, don't say anything to others. And if it really serves no purpose except to perpetuate that bit of gossip you heard or created yourself, *don't say anything at all.*

And someone beginning the conversation with "It's not gossip, it's just a prayer concern," means it is just gossip. Stop it in its tracks before it has a chance to spread any further.

FIFTY-SEVEN

Make One Good Decision and Build on it. If you can make five good decisions in a row, you can change your life.

(Roger Lengyel)

If you've burned down your house – or burned all your bridges – and find yourself sitting in an ash heap, don't mourn the loss long. Get up and ask God for that "one good decision" and step out in faith knowing the Eternal Carpenter will give you all the next building blocks you need to rebuild with indestructible material. Make five good decisions, and watch your life flourish with God's blessings!

FIFTY-EIGHT

Water your own lawn

You've heard the expression, "The grass is always greener on the other side of the hill." We always think if we had this or that thing, another job, a better house, spouse, or car that we would be happier. We look with envy at the person who is popular, has more recognition or is more talented, and we grow discontent and bitter.

But if the grass looks greener on the other side of the hill, just water your own lawn. Start by being thankful for all you have – which is thousands of times more than 99% of the world has. Pray for that powerful discipline – *contentment*. Paul said, "…I have learned, in whatsoever state I am, therewith to be content. I know both how to be abased, and I know how to abound: every where and in all things I am instructed both to be full and to be hungry, both to abound and to suffer need." (Phil. 4:-11-12)

No matter what, Paul was thankful for what He had, content and at peace with what God had given him. With that, he and Silas turned a prison into songs of praise and God opened the prison doors.

FIFTY-NINE

If you're real, people don't care if you're relevant.

There's a lot of talk about "authenticity" and "relevancy" and "relational ministry" these days, and largely, it's often just fluffy words but no substance. If you're busy trying to convince people how authentic and relevant you are, then you probably aren't.

Kids especially can tell if an adult or a youth pastor is trying to impress them with "cool" and "relevant." Kids don't want you to be *like* them. They want you to be *better* than them. That's why they like superheroes.

Relevant is concerned with how we look; real is a matter of the heart, someone who loves, bleeds, feels, and yet is solid, determined, and ready to help people survive and spiritually thrive in this dark and dangerous world.

SIXTY

Love is always having to say you're sorry

There was a sappy romantic movie decades ago whose tagline was, "Love is never having to say you're sorry." I laughed when I heard it because as a Christian, love is *always* having to say you're sorry. Even when you're right. Pride makes us stand our ground in marriage and friendships and refuses to apologize or admit wrong. But being right and making sure others know it, even if it damages a relationship, is a fool's response. Sometimes it doesn't matter whether you're right. Just say you're sorry. Humble yourself. In the long run, your relationship is more important than your rightness.

SIXTY-ONE

God has called us to be faithful, not successful.

"Seekest thou great things for thyself? Seek them not." (Jeremiah 45:5)

Modern ministry is designed toward success, numbers, a following, likes on Facebook.

Jesus had few real followers, yet He accomplished the salvation of the lost on the cross.

Follow the footsteps of Jesus. It doesn't matter if you are "successful" in human eyes. What matters is, did you obey Him, were you faithful in the little, did you trust Him in it all?

Human success looks at the outward. God sees faithfulness as the ultimate success in His people.

SIXTY-TWO

Preparation is everything

Those entering ministry are often frustrated by delays, struggles, failures, and battles.

Don't despair. It is all part of God's work in you. Preparation is difficult but so necessary for the success of what He has called you to do. Even when painful, embrace the process. The Father knows what He is doing, and the end result of preparation will be great and enduring fruit.

SIXTY-THREE

Never sacrifice the eternal on the altar of the temporary.
(Unknown)

We live in an instant everything world where our worldly wants and desires are just seconds away from fulfillment. Our sinful flesh desires instant satisfaction and gratification, and it takes Jesus to "crucify the flesh with the affections and lusts thereof." (Galatians 5:24)

Especially in relationships, it is easy to pursue someone based on attraction or even lust and throw away our walk for a moment's pleasure, or marry someone we know is not God's choice for us because we are just lonely and do not trust that God can find us the person that will be His best for us.

There is so much at stake in making right, good decisions. Don't sacrifice the eternal blessings God wants to give you for a moment's gratification or a substitute for His best.

SIXTY-FOUR

Neither youth nor age is an impediment to God's work. If God calls you to it, He will give you everything you need to fulfill it.

There is wisdom in age, and vitality in youth. But there can be both in it all. God called young people to serve Him, like Jeremiah: "Do not say 'I am only a child.'" (Jeremiah 1:7) And Timothy: "Let no man despise your youth." (1 Timothy 4:12) And God called Abram, Moses, and Zechariah the High Priest in advanced age for His purposes. My scriptural role model is Caleb, who said, "I am this day 85 years old. As yet I am as strong this day that Moses sent me: as my strength was then, even so is my strength now, for war, both to go out, and to come in." (Joshua 14:10-11) Our bodies may limit us but may God give us the heart of Caleb to be 100% in our spirit, our prayers, and our service all the way to the end.

God can call you and use you, regardless of your age.

SIXTY-FIVE

In your whole life, you will likely be able to count your very closest friends on both hands. (Doris Shumate)

This was a little counsel that my spiritual mother gave to me in my second year of being a believer. I didn't like it. I wanted friends and loved ones – lots of them – for a lifetime. It was the naiveté and ambition of youth that created that desire, and her words were not comforting at all.

But they have been absolutely true.

Though many people have come and gone, many did not remain. But oh, the blessing of having that handful for a lifetime, ones that have suffered the waves of violent storms and adverse circumstances, testings and disagreements, distance and time-lapses in between fellowship, and yet here they are. Those few are worth all the "thousand closest friends" you think you have when you are young who turn out to simply be people for who you were simply a passing novelty friendship.

I will never forget attending the 50th wedding anniversary of my spiritual father and Pastor Rick

Howard, and as precious friends from over decades came to celebrate, Rick's sweet wife Anita quoted – and sang – the first words from a very old song from another era:

> Make new friends, but keep the old;
> Those are silver, these are gold.
> New-made friendships, like new wine,
> Age will mellow and refine.
> Friendships that have stood the test-
> Time and change-are surely best;
> Brow may wrinkle, hair grow gray;
> Friendship never knows decay.
> For 'mid old friends, tried and true,
> Once more we our youth renew.
> But old friends, alas! may die;
> New friends must their place supply.
> Cherish friendship in your breast-
> New is good, but old is best;
> Make new friends, but keep the old;
> Those are silver, these are gold.
> - Joseph Parry

Choose your friends carefully. May God grant you golden friends to last a lifetime and on into eternity!

SIXTY-SIX
There's A Meadow in Every Flower
(Amy Carmichael)

Missionary Amy Carmichael dedicated her entire life to the rescuing of children in India from slavery and prostitution. She was dedicated to the Word of God, studying it, teaching it, and living it. In the course of her writings, she was so profoundly moved by the infinite depth of the Word of God that she made this statement.

Have you ever read a scripture, having read it several times before and suddenly it becomes alive, and you see in it a truth that you never saw before? So is the Word of God. In every gem, there are a trillion facets. In every flower, there is a meadow. In every verse, there is the eternal truth of God that never gets old, nor fails to teach us new things.

SIXTY-SEVEN

Don't choose people who are eager to lead. Choose those who are called to lead.

In our age, it is far too easy to choose leaders based on charisma rather than calling. Choose servants with humble hearts who are likely not looking to lead.

As a friend once prayed, "God, help us to make sure we have appointed those that You have anointed."

SIXTY-EIGHT

The reward for being responsible is more responsibility.
(Tim Gamwell)

If you're looking for lots of perks and cool stuff in ministry, you may be disappointed. If you accomplish the small thing Jesus asked you to do, He is going to hand you a whole lot more to do. And that's a good thing.

More of Him, less of us. Dependent on Him to be responsible for whatever He entrusts us with knowing that in the end, He will give us all we need to see it through.

SIXTY-NINE

We are called to proclaim, not to explain.

The world loves to argue and debate. But we need to avoid being entangled with distracting tactics of the enemy when trying to lead people to Jesus.

Stay on message. We don't have to answer the innumerable questions that an unbeliever may bring up in objecting to the message of Jesus, for the questions are rarely motivated by a desire for truth, but rather a desire to avoid surrender to the Lordship of Jesus. Do not be distracted: proclaim the message simply and scripturally, and the power of God will do its saving work.

SEVENTY

The Elijah Burnout Principle

Elijah was a powerful man of God who did what no one else had done in ages – he confronted the prophets of Baal, called on God to demonstrate who was God, destroyed the prophets and their altars, and all of that publicly. What a victory! He feared the prophets of Baal not one bit.

But when Queen Jezebel learned of the ruination of her precious Baal priests, she swore to kill Elijah. And so, he ran.

WHAT?!

Why would a great man of God who didn't fear hundreds of murderous idol worshippers run from one idolatrous queen?

In fact, he ran far away, sat down under a tree and asked God to let him die.

What happened?

I think Elijah may have succumbed to the H.A.L.T. effect. It stands for "Hungry, angry, lonely and tired." He was just burned out.

Operating under the power of God and proclaiming truth in a hostile setting is draining and exhausting at times. Elijah gave it all at Mount Carmel, and it may have just all hit him at once at the sound of Jezebel's threats.

But what did God do? Chide him? Ask him why he failed in faith?

No. He gave him a nap and a snack. He sent an angel to wake him up and feed him and let him rest. His problem wasn't a failure of faith but more likely a natural result of being spent by all that he did.

Ministry can be exhausting, and we need to be careful to take care of ourselves. If you find yourself getting fearful, losing perspective, becoming irritated with people and praying despairing prayers (God, I thought you called me! Why did I even agree to go into ministry?) what you need is to HALT. Get off the fast-food track and eat better. Pray through the building anger you might be harboring. Find some good friends to spend time with. *And get some rest.*

"I'd rather burn out than rust out," a ministry friend once told me. I told him about an old VW I had that I just ran ragged. I was very young and didn't know what the nice little red flashing light was on my dashboard until my engine blew up. It was the oil light. I had ignored it until the engine ran out of oil and now, I had no car.

Listen to the red lights God sends us to warn us to take care of ourselves. While burning out sounds noble, isn't it better to keep your life and ministry well-maintained to make sure you can go the distance?

SEVENTY-ONE
The End Will Explain All Things
(Amy Carmichael)

In the midst of all the blessings we know as believers, life is also often marred by tragedies, losses, heartaches, grief and inexplicable difficulties and trials. At those times our human hearts cry, "Why, Father? I don't understand!" It is a cry God does not reject. Sometimes we will have answers; but many times, we will not, and that is where the words above have spoken deeply to me. One day, it will all make sense. One day, God will explain the whys. Like a Persian rug or a tapestry, the backside of it looks like a mess of disconnected threads and meaningless patterns. But one day, God will turn over the tapestry of our lives and show us the glorious picture, the magnificent weaving of eternal meaning and beauty He was able to create with our lives.

Don't despair if the answers do not come. It is human to cry, "Why? I don't understand!" But add to that the words of faith that will put the unbearable questions into His hand: "I don't understand. **But I trust You, Jesus.**" And one day, you will see the purpose of it all.

SEVENTY-TWO

If the Earth is this beautiful under a curse, imagine how beautiful it will be when the curse is removed.

(Doris Shumate)

Sometimes we get so bogged down with the darkness and the evil in this world that it is hard to keep our perspective. I think that is why we go on vacation, looking for that beautiful place, that mountain jewel, that desert Oasis, that Caribbean or Hawaiian escape because it reminds us that not everything is ugly in this world. There is still beauty and wonder and awe.

One day as we were sitting with my spiritual Mom overlooking the breathtaking green valley of Topanga Canyon, breathing in the heady smell of trees and flowers and the sea breeze wafting through the canyon, bringing with it fog and the intoxicating smell of ocean and sand, Doris reminded us of this truth. Yes, this earth is beautiful, in some places so beautiful that it makes your heart ache. But all this is a beauty marred by the curse of man's sin and wickedness. But when that curse is removed – when He comes and makes a new heaven and a new earth, well, we can't even begin to comprehend how spectacularly beautiful it will be. And as she used to quote, eye has not seen, nor ear heard, nor has it entered into the heart of man what God has prepared for those who love Him. (1 Corinthians 2:9)

In all the pain and suffering, loss and grief of life that mixes in with the joy and hope of being a believer in Jesus, it helps to remember this. The best of this world is merely a tiny sneak preview of the glorious wonders to come when He returns and sets the world aright.

SEVENTY-THREE

Churches used to put the youth and children in the basement of the church. We need to put the adults in the basement and the children and youth in the main sanctuary with the windows.

(Rick C Howard)

I'm fairly sure when Pastor Rick said this recently, he didn't fully know how profoundly true it is. It seems like nearly all of our attention is focused on adult ministry while we relegate "junior ministries" like youth and children to a back room and hire a few people to manage or entertain them. Many churches really don't take them very seriously.

Let them sit with us often. Give them windows to see the great vastness of God's Kingdom, knowing that they are the future of the church. We need to afford them every glimpse into their part of that future that we can.

SEVENTY-FOUR

The attack on the work of God is always against the person that God has called to build that work.
(Rick C. Howard)

No work of God is done without His people to make it happen. Nehemiah was called to build, and the attacks from the enemies of God's work were leveled at him consistently and viciously in an attempt to get him to stop.

The devil attacks you through your finances, your computers, or people around you. He's attacking you and using things and people around you to do so, trying to wear you out and get you to abandon your post.

I once spoke with a pastor of a Native American congregation who told me of a medicine man who had gotten saved and came to speak at their church. "Do you send curses and attacks against me to get me to quit?" "No," the man confessed. "We send curses and attacks against your people so that if enough of them leave, you will eventually quit and leave."

If God has called you to build, be prepared for attacks on everything and everyone around you, and understand that it is all designed to get you to come down off the wall and stop your work. Stay steady. Outlast the attacks. God will give you all you need to finish what He has called you to do.

SEVENTY-FIVE
Ishmael often comes before Isaac

When we are seeking direction, don't just jump at the first thing that comes along. Abraham was so anxious to see God's promise fulfilled that he devised a way in the flesh to carry out that promise. It created conflict, contention and delay. He got the first son, but he did not obtain the promise through him. It came through Isaac, his second son born by miracle of God.

Satan sometimes sends his "Ishmael" to you first to tempt you into not waiting for God's open door. Don't get impatient. Wait. You may find that the Ishmael you were sent was an attempt to keep you from the fulfillment of God's plan for you.

SEVENTY-SIX
The shame about judgment day is not what we did or didn't do, but what we could have become if we had truly let Jesus be Lord of our life.

(Rick C. Howard)

We become so focused on our sins and failures, weaknesses and struggles, on petty things and doctrinal disputes, the cares of this world and the desire for more that we miss offering our total surrender to His Lordship and letting Him have full control of our lives and our future.

D.L. Moody said, "The world has yet to see what God can do with a man fully consecrated to Him. who is completely and totally dedicated to Him, and I aim to be that man." I want to be that person too.

What about you?

SEVENTY-SEVEN

We are immortal until our work on earth is done.

(George Whitefield)

He who has every hair on our head numbered, who doesn't even allow a sparrow to fall without Him, knows the very days of your life. And you can be sure that until God has finished with everything He has called to do through you, in you and with you, you are secure and can rest in His loving hands. The time of your departure is neither random nor purposeless. And until that day comes, give your 100% fearlessly to God's plan for your life with confidence that He who knows you from the day you were born, will also attend to your Homegoing when the time comes. And it won't come one second before *He* allows it.

SEVENTY-EIGHT

I could do great things if I wasn't so distracted doing unimportant things.

Life is so full of distractions. With every new social media app, binge-series or YouTube video we've got to watch, we get more caught up in things that don't really matter, at the expense of what really does matter. We need to be asking, "In the light of eternity, how is this activity going to speak for me on judgment day? What spiritual value does it have?

I'm not saying don't do fun things. I'm saying we all get a set amount of time here, and the devil is very good at trying to make sure you're caught up in worldly things and trivial activities, so you won't focus on prayer, study, fellowship and making a difference for Jesus in this fallen world.

Do a life "downsize." Trim the empty activity fat. Ask God to help you invest your time – a most precious and limited resource – where it will matter most for eternity.

We all have to do laundry and take out the trash, sure. But don't let all the busy work and distractions keep you from what really matters.

I had a dear friend who had spoken for years about finishing a screenplay she had been writing, and it was one that would have had a great impact for the Kingdom. As I sat at her funeral, I mourned that she never got it done. It's not a criticism. It was a warning to me about not putting off what is most important to do.

SEVENTY-NINE

Sometimes God will give you what you want. And you will regret that you insisted that He let you have it.

You can beg God enough about something you want, fully knowing it's not God's best for you and may not even be good for you, and He may just give it to you.

"And He gave them their request; but sent leanness into their soul." (Psalm 106:15)

Someone once said that God gives the very best to those who leave the choice to Him. He knows what is best. But this verse is very plain: If the only way God can teach you is by letting you have that thing that He knows is not good for you, He will. And your soul will grow lean and spiritually empty until you turn again to Him.

EIGHTY

Do the thing that is in front of you to do. "What is in your hand?"

There are times in the lives of all believers and kingdom servants when we seem to be at a stopping point. Your plans are not working out; you are wondering why doors aren't opening, and you don't seem to be being used by the Lord. How do you persevere through these downtimes? Don't worry about tomorrow or the next day. Just do what is in front of you to do that day, every day, even if it seems useless and fruitless to you. Do it for Jesus and in rejoicing, and the doors will open when the time is right.

"And whatever you do, do it heartily, as to the Lord and not to men." (Colossians 3:23)

EIGHTY-ONE

God tailors your trials to fit your needs

(Unknown)

I am fearfully and wonderfully made. (Psalm 139) God knows me inside and out, past, present, and future, and knows which trials are perfectly suited for me to make me more like Jesus. Don't curse the trials. Thank Him that if He allowed it, greater good will come from it. (Romans 8:28) It's His promise.

EIGHTY-TWO

You can't catch a fish hoping that you might

(Michael Kelly Blanchard)

I first heard this in a song by the amazing poet-songwriter singer Michael Kelly Blanchard, and it made me laugh and stuck with me. I don't know if it originated with him, or if it was, as the song explained, wise advice from an older fisherman.

But it's 100% true. Procrastination is the plague of our age. Stop putting off the things you are called to do, or feel like you'd like to accomplish.

There's no better time to do those things than today. You don't have any guarantee of tomorrow. Get to it!

EIGHTY-THREE

If you aren't accepted by those who should accept you, you will go with anyone who will accept you.

This is a good bit of understanding, especially for parents and believers. The need for love and acceptance runs very deep. Be the ones to provide that so that your children, or people in our churches and youth groups, won't drink from poison waters simply out of desperation for a cool drink of human acceptance and love.

EIGHTY-FOUR

Tell me who you're with, and I will tell you who you are.

In Spanish, "Dime con quién andas y te diré quién eres." The friends and company we keep say more about us than about our words claiming to follow Jesus.

If you prefer the company of your party-loving friends or secular work associates to the neglecting of fellowship with believers, it's time to reexamine the level of your commitment to Jesus and your willingness to follow Him, even if it costs you relationships. "Evil communications (companionship) corrupts good matters (ethics, character). (1 Corinthians 15:33)

Don't let bad relationships mar the face of Jesus' witness in your life.

EIGHTY-FIVE

What is that to thee?

Jesus, John 21:22

It's in our human nature to want to meddle in other people's lives, be upset by their decisions or even envious of their successes. We may even have a genuine concern for people, and we ask what God was doing with that person and why.

The story in John is crucial. After Jesus was resurrected and had just eaten breakfast with his disciples, Peter said, "What about John? What's going to happen to him?"

"What is that to thee?" Jesus answered. "Follow thou me."

So many times, I have been tempted to meddle or complain about someone or try to question why they're doing what they are doing, and I always hear Jesus saying this to me. "What is that to thee? Follow thou me."

It's God's loving version of, "That's none of your business. Just tend to your own walk with Me."

EIGHTY-SIX

Vas you there?

(Doris Shumate)

This came from an old radio comedy show. The main character, Baron von Munchausen, would tell these elaborate, hardly believable stories, and his partner couldn't believe it. "Vas you there, Charlie?" The Baron would ask.

My spiritual mother told this story in reference to gossip and stories that were going around about another person. "Vas you there?" she often said when we strayed into dangerous areas of discussing other people's sins or faults – just plain gossip.

In other words, don't gossip or speak ill of people if you don't know them. Don't judge situations if you are not personally involved and if you don't know what is really going on.

Next time you're tempted to spread a rumor, ask yourself, "Vas you there?" Do you know for certain that what you heard is true? No? Then set a guard on your lips and leave it in God's hands.

EIGHTY-SEVEN

The Gospel is for the one

I am thankful for the big crusades and the mass events that lead people to Jesus.

But ultimately, it's not about numbers and crowds. The Gospel is for the one. It's about the one lost sheep the Shepherd left the crowd to rescue. It's about the one lost coin in the house. It's about the one hurting heart, the one widow, the one orphan, the one drug addict, the one special needs child. We often say, "If you were the only person in the universe, Jesus would have come and died for you." And it's true.

While we are "winning souls," remember that each one is precious in the sight of the Father and should receive all the care and love we can provide them in His precious Name.

EIGHTY-EIGHT
It's not who goes to the prom…it's who shows up for the reunion

It's always awesome to see people come to Jesus, especially in church meetings or Christian concerts or other evangelistic events.

And you want all of them to go the distance with Jesus.

Some start out well and end up falling halfway through the race.

Some start out slow and stumbling and finish strong.

I remember years ago when a famous Hollywood celebrity had found Jesus, and as we discussed it, a friend said, "Let's have the party two years from now." That's when I started to understand that sometimes people start out with a lot of fire and energy and promise. We promote them and put them in front of the crowds instead of discipling them and making sure they have what it takes to stand strong, and they sometimes don't make it the whole distance but end up falling back into their old ways. Yet others may seem they won't even make the first lap but end up being a long-distance runner and finisher.

For whatever reasons this is so – even while we rejoice in someone coming to Jesus – it's not who comes to the party but who makes it to the reunion that matters.

EIGHTY-NINE

Respond, don't react.

Again, this is a discipline that takes a lifetime. But in every testy situation, challenging or rancorous conversation or negative exchange, what matters is that we do not react in a knee-jerk fleshly way, but that we take a deep breath and respond in a way that would represent the love and character of Jesus the best.

You'll probably fail more at this than succeed. But keep at it. Keep in in the forefront of your mind when you find yourself in situations that can be volatile and hurtful if not handled the Jesus way. "A soft answer turns away wrath, but grievous words stir up anger." (Proverbs 15:1)

NINETY

You have to earn the right to speak into someone's life

Years ago, there was a monstrous movement in the church we called the "Shepherding Movement." A handful of men set up a system of submission/authority in churches that ended up destroying many young believers.

I believe in the biblical principles of submission and authority. But we must understand its limitations. We have a responsibility to watch out for the flock and defend them from wolves. We are required to confront sin when we see it, especially if it affects others.

But we are not given the role of telling someone where they should live, what job they should take or who they should marry (as long as they are a believer.) These were some of the excesses of the Shepherding Movement. If someone tries to control your spiritual life that way, *run!*

As God's shepherds, we must understand that we don't have a right to demand that someone let us dictate the details of their personal life. My jurisdiction ends when that person leaves my church walls – unless they *ask* me to speak into their lives. And I have to earn the right to do so, by my consistent care, my love and my demonstration of Jesus in my relationship with them.

NINETY-ONE

It's not the mountain ahead of you; it's the rock in your shoe. The rock the hammer can't break, time and tide will wear away.

We will all be faced with big challenges, and God will help us to meet them all.

But it is the little things that we need to be wary of, for they have the potential to drain the spiritual life out of us. Knowing that this is a long-distance race, we need to make sure we are prepared to go the distance. Daniel says of our enemy, "…he shall wear out the saints of the most High…" (Daniel 7:25) Do all that you can to eliminate those things that the enemy throws your way just to wear you out. Rest. Eat well. Pray much. Read the Word daily. Those are the antidotes to the wearing out that the enemy attempts in our daily lives.

NINETY-TWO

Responsibility is our Response to His Ability (Unknown)

What God calls you to, He will equip you for and give you all you need to carry it out. "For it is God who works in you both to will and to do His good pleasure." (Philippians 2:13)

Say yes, be ready and leave the rest to Him.

NINETY-THREE

The last part of the race can be the hardest.

Something I was not taught in Bible School was that, excluding the return of Jesus or going to be with Him at a young age, the last part of the journey can be the most difficult. This is not to be feared, as our loving Father has made provision for our entire lives, from birth to old age. But we should be aware that we have a very real enemy who knows he is running out of time to derail you, and he will do all he can to make the last run treacherous if he can.

Knowing this, understand that it is not a time to slacken your hand or coast into glory. Quite the opposite – you must daily armor up to prevent the enemy from taking you down.

There is no need for defeat in that final race. Be alert, stay close to Jesus, and finish your course with joy!

NINETY-FOUR

You can't battle Satan if you've got his toys in your back pocket.

Before you decide to step out into the real spiritual warfare arena or undertake a great work or ministry for Jesus, make sure you aren't hiding or participating in Satan's sins and worldly flesh pursuits. He'll call you out right away and send you running away from the battlefield whimpering.

NINETY-FIVE

Just because there's a need, doesn't mean you are supposed to fill it.

We had an inside joke years ago when we got cornered in church and were pressured into being involved in some activity, project, or outreach. "I got voluntold," we'd say.

There are always a multitude of needs both inside and outside the church. One can easily attempt to meet every need that comes your way until you are overwhelmed because needs never stop. You will soon reach burnout, and then suffer with the guilt you feel because you committed to doing so much and end up failing to do most of it.

Before you respond to a need or volunteer, first ask yourself whether it is something God has called you to do. (This doesn't apply to lazy Christians who haven't lifted a finger for the Kingdom or the church in years…) God hasn't asked us to do everything; only do those things He commissions you to do.

NINETY-SIX

Never deny in darkness what you know to be true in the light.

(V. Raymond Edman)

All of us will go through dark times in our walk. Jesus said in the world we would have tribulation. Paul's apostleship was marked with great suffering, and martyrdom was the rule of the day for believers.

The scriptures are full of accounts of God's people passing through great hardships before they obtained victory, from Joseph being put in a dank prison, to Job losing everything, to Jeremiah being stuck in a hole in the ground.

It is what we do in those moments that decide the value of those moments. Was God good, gracious, loving, caring, and protecting you before you entered your dark night? He is all of that still. The devil will do his best to get you to forget those truths, to get you to doubt God and His loving plan for your life, as he comes and hisses in your ear, "Where is your God *now*?"

David had the answer: "If I say, 'Surely the

darkness shall cover me; even the night shall be light about me." (Psalm 139:11)

He is still the same loving Father in the dark as He is when you were surrounded by light and blessings. His promises are still true. Trust Him, deny not what you knew to be true in that time of blessing! Let the dark times do God's perfecting work in you, and proclaim the truth in the midst of even the darkest circumstances, and He will carry you through.

NINETY-SEVEN

Congratulations – you made the radar!

"Why is being a Christian so hard? I never struggled when I was an unbeliever. And why do so many other Christians have it so easy? I made a commitment to follow Jesus, and all hell broke loose after that!"

Congratulations. You made the enemy's radar. You see, he is not threatened by Christians who do nothing for the Gospel, whose commitment is a Sunday-only, Christmas and Easter one, and in-name-only Christians. The devil is perfectly content to leave them alone. They are no threat.

But once you decide to be all-in for Jesus and hand it all over to Him - your future, your relationships, your possessions, and your will – you will come up on the devil's radar. He will go into action to try to take you out.

Getting attacked and things getting tough and embattled isn't a sign you're doing something wrong, but that you've moved in the right direction toward true purpose and effectiveness in Jesus.

Welcome to the battlefield!

NINETY-EIGHT

We will be very surprised on judgment day who made it that we thought wouldn't and who didn't we thought would.

(Rick C. Howard)

How quick we are to judge another person's salvation. The big trend right now is talking about "false conversions," people who prayed "to receive Jesus in their hearts" but aren't really saved.

Perhaps. But we should be very careful about making those judgments. "Who are you to judge another man's servant?" (Romans 14:4) Jesus said there would be those who claimed to do miracles and other things on judgment day and he will tell them, "Depart from me, I never knew you." (Matthew 7:23)

We do know no one gets to heaven without Jesus. And we know salvation is a gift of God, not of works. So before we declare with certainty who is saved and who is not, we need to stand back. Only God knows the heart, and He judges the content of our hearts. I think there will be plenty of people who live morally, mouth the words but never met

Jesus. And I believe there are others who gave their lives to Jesus but struggle and sin and fall but are still His. I don't want to be the one making those judgments, and neither do you.

And we never know what happens in those last moments of a person's life. I suspect there will be a few thieves on the cross standing in white robes that we would have never given a chance to make it in.

NINETY-NINE

If someone gets your goat, it's because you've got a goat to get.

(Dale Walker)

"She made me so angry!" "He made me do that." "You always make me act that way!"

No. Nobody can make you feel anything or do anything. As believers, God doesn't let us get away with blaming others for our reactions. We take spiritual responsibility for everything we do or say, without becoming Saul, whose famous line was, "The people made me do it." (1 Samuel 15:21)

If someone "triggers" you, it's because you are triggerable. If someone acts out in the flesh and you act back and lash back, it's because your own flesh is still alive and well. You still have a goat to get. So get that goat of the flesh, when someone gets your goat, and recognize that God has allowed it so you can see how much you are still in need of crucifying the flesh in your own life. Take that ugly flesh goat to the cross and say, "Jesus, I am sorry. It doesn't matter what THEY did or said. What matters is what I do, and I am asking you to help me lay this on the cross and crucify it."

Lord, in all things, let love be my response. Let grace be my answer. Let truth – Your truth, not my own self-defensive instincts, be the only thing I respond with.

ONE-HUNDRED

What God reveals, He heals

Don't ever fear the exposure of the hidden things of your heart. We all have pockets of sin, darkness and pain we keep carefully concealed from others for fear of judgment, rejection or misunderstanding. And that which hides in darkness grows and touches everything in our lives.

Let the Father bring the hidden things into His light. He doesn't want to humiliate you nor shame you. He wants to deliver and heal you. If possible, find a trusted friend that you can share anything with in confidence and let them pray with you and walk it out with you. "Confess your faults one to another and pray for each other that you might be healed." (James 5:16) And remember that we don't have a High Priest that cannot be touched by our struggles; but was in *all things* tempted like us, but didn't sin. (Hebrews 4:15)

He knows how to bring you out and set you free. But you have to stop hiding. After all, He knows it all anyway. In bringing your heart to Him in brokenness and need, He will lift you out of your bondage. What He reveals, He heals; what you hide, destructively grows in the darkness.

"Search me, O God, and know my heart; try me, and know my thoughts: And see if there be any wicked way in me, and lead me in the way everlasting." (Psalm 139:23-24)

ONE HUNDRED-ONE

You're better than me

I had the honor of shepherding a group of young people for seven years. We walked together for seven mission trips from Navajo reservations to big youth camps, we celebrated birthdays and holidays and wept together when one of our own passed away. I have precious memories for a lifetime, and they are still very much part of my life though I am no longer their youth pastor.

Early on, I read a scripture that seemed to define my heart for them. From that came an expression that I shared with them, and somehow it caught on: "You're better than me."

The scriptures say, "Let each esteem the other better than themselves." (Philippians 2:3) A humble heart looks at the other and considers them first, honors them and treats them with the heart of a servant. So I attempted to do with these young lives God gifted me to serve, and so they did to me and each other. Before long, it became kind of our spiritual motto: "You're better than me," one would say. "No, you're better than me," the other replied.

"You're better than me." If we see each other that way, our hearts will remain humble and tender, and we can truly fulfill Jesus' words, "He that humbles himself as this little child, the same is the greatest in the Kingdom of heaven." (Matthew 18:4)

I dedicate this book to all those I was – and am still – blessed to shepherd. Thank you all for letting me serve you all these amazing years! You truly are better than me!

BOOKS BY GREGORY R REID

NOBODY'S ANGEL

NOBODY'S ANGEL: THE TTUF INTERVIEWS (WITH JAMES JOSEPH FIRE)

TROJAN CHURCH

WAR OF THE AGES

A CRY IN THE WILDERNESS

HEALING IN HIS WINGS

THE COLOR OF PAIN

TREASURE FROM THE MASTER'S HEART

NEHEMIAH: REBUILDING THE RUINS

STRAY CATS AND OTHER STORIES

SILENCE AND THE DISTANCE BETWEEN US

ABOUT THE AUTHOR

Dr. Gregory Reid is an ordained minister with American Evangelistic Association and a retired private investigator who has trained over 100 criminal justice departments nationwide on occult crimes and crimes against children. He is actively involved in youth ministry and youth outreach as well as conducting spiritual warfare training at churches nationwide.

www.gregoryreid.com

legendaryseeker@gmail.com

Made in the USA
Monee, IL
17 February 2020